Dance of A Thousand Muses

By

Devyn Barat

Crystal Dreams Publishing
W1227 East County Rd ABerlin, WI
54923

Acknowledgements

Copious thanks to Sylence Campbell, Vauren Davidson, Mark Nelson, Heathyre Perara & the Shadow Poets Society for their encouragement and support.

Art is Magick!

Art is Expression. Art is Philosophy. Art is Spirituality.
Art is akin to taking a big magnifying glass to yourself or to the world around you and saying, "Hey people, take a look at this!" Art should make you THINK; should make you FEEL.

Art isn't limited to the mediums of the artist: words, paint, clay, stone, movement, etc. Art is infinite. Art is everywhere!

Art is you!
People are art. Nature is art.

Art is beautiful and art is ugly (and even then beautiful).

Life *itself* is art.
Life *creates* art.

Godde is the Great Artist.

Some of us "get it," and some don't.
We are the ones who see magick in something mundane that goes unnoticed in daily life and hold up that magnifying glass so those who don't "get it," might.

Perhaps that's part of it too, to try to show others
what we see: to share the consciousness; to
experience the magick; to uncover the mystery; to
pull back the veil and see the hand of Godde that
paints our lives with every stroke.

Poetry is art.
There are poems lurking in all things.
All it takes is vision to see the muse and gain the
inspiration.
Every poem is a revelation.

**Muses dance everywhere…and inspiration is
divine!**

Anon…
Devyn Barat
Magickal Poet

A Theatrical Act of Creation

Inspire me, O Muses!
So that my emotions may flow
From this pen, and here in words,
This playwright's heart be shown!
And there - upon the stage -
O let me see
A parade of emotions;
A dance of humanity.
Let it be expressed in rhyme and song.
And let it be danced
If words would be wrong.
Let all nine of the Ladies
Of Parnassus & Helicon Peak
Inspire this creation
Of the Arts I seek.
Let there be dance & song;
Let it be comic & tragic;
Emotional & inspirational;
And, above all, magick!
For when the words that are written
Upon the script's page
Are translated lovingly
To the living stage,
It is humanity
That is celebrated.
When the Arts come together as one
It is Life that is created!
So let there be light!

Apollo, strike Your Lyre!
Muses, fill my creation
With inspirational fire!
Let my artistic work
Breathe life on the stage!
And let the audience, in their seats,
Be uncontrollably engaged.
And when they empathize as one,
And laughter & tears fill their hearts,
Then - only then - is my job done.
Then this poet has done his part.
Let me look upon the stage,
As a proud parent would,
And let me say to myself,
"It is good!"

A Thousand Muses Dance

A thousand muses dance before me
The world is full of inspiration
Every sense frantically gathering
The kindling of creation

There's a song in a sigh
A tale in a glance
And a young girl's walk
Turns into a dance

A painting springs
From a smile full of charms
And a poem is born
Within a lover's arms

This is the mettle
From which art is made
Divine inspiration
In a mundane charade

Addiction

I'm not ashamed to admit it,
I may have an addiction.
I cannot withstand
The irresistible temptation
Of your appealing lips;
Soft, gentle, velvety.
Without forming words
They seductively call me
For my own to kiss,
And to hold an embrace
Lips paired together
In love and in grace.
No amount of kisses
Will satisfy my desire
For in kissing you
My lips are set on fire
With passionate ecstasy.
I can't explain the sensation
But without it I hunger,
Dying of starvation.
Save me from withdrawal
And suffering cricks.
Kiss me again
And give me my fix.

Affectionate Embraces

Arms & arms
'Round two bodies to hold
Hands in hands
Gentle fingers enfold
Lips to lips
And face to face
Love to love
In each embrace
Trading affection
Kiss for kiss
Touch for touch
And bliss for bliss
Contact made
As if to bless
Expressing love
In each caress

<u>Again</u>

Again, you fall silent
No reason given why
Stagnant with a hush
My trust begins to die

My heart you strung along
Now the strings you cut
The door that was opening
You have now slammed shut

Along Comes Spring

Along comes Spring
Rising from ashen Winter
In an outbreak of Color
Painting the Earth a Rainbow
With Nature's Pallet
'Till the organic Spectrum
Reaches its chromatically blinding climax

Aphrodite

Born of Foam
And rising up from the sea
The Graces attend Thee
Goddess of Love
And Lover of Laughter
Who delights in side-glances
And mischievous smiles

Apollo

Far-Seeing Protector of Truth
Keeper of the Muses
And of the Arts
Strike Your Lyre
Shine Your Light
Inspire my pen

As They Slip Away...

Looking at the Sunrise
  A new day has come about
    Another day I have everything
      But your love which I'm
        without

Thinking of your sweet kiss
  And the feel of your caress
    Reminds me of the times
      I only knew happiness

Looking outside the window
  Waiting for you to appear
    Brings a tear of sadness
      Wishing you were here

Doomed to hide within these walls
  For countless hours and days
    Praying that this pain I feel
      Is just a passing phase

Sitting awake with fear all night
  `Till the redeeming Sunrise
    When anxiety is wiped away
      From wide and tearing eyes

Counting the weeks, one by one
  Day after passing day
    A tear is shed regretfully
      As they slip away

Aware

We become aware of ourselves
Through each other

The Lord and Lady become aware of each other
Through us

The Universe becomes aware of Itself
Through our Love

Be Kind

Those lips, those sweet, sweet lips
(Though their sweetness I've yet to know)
Tempt me with a pucker and a pout
And more and more desirable grow

Your lips will dissolve me in my steps
Melting me with your kiss
Warming me to my depths
In a way that's not amiss

Oh! I dream of your kiss daily
So, if within your heart, you find
Some sparks of love for me
Then please kiss me, be kind

Beyond Words

I love you beyond words
But I must express this

My love won't go unheard
You will taste it in my kiss

Bleed to Death

I recoil from your touch
What once was pleasure
Now inflicts pain
Memories cut like razors
The wounds you delivered
Causing my heart
To slowly
bleed
to
death

Vows undone
Promises broken
Dishonesty dances
The line of truth
My trust in you
Lies
bleeding
to
death

My most intimate lover
Now in the guise of a stranger
Fading away
Like a dissolving dream
And blown away
By the relentless wind
My last hope
Left
bleeding
to
death

Will my wounds ever heal?
Will we restore our hearts?
My love
Has
bled
to
death

Bleeding Heart

My wounded heart goes on loving you
enduring despite betrayal.
Is it limitless love or
foolish perseverance?
Though eternally
bleeding to death,
it knows not
how to
die.

Blood from Stone

Cold stone; magma within
Silence without; inside a din
Shrouded dreams and shouting fears
Dry emotions, invisible tears
Fingers of phobia, wrapped up tight
Grasping firm with all its might
How long can one, this torture, endure
Before, crying loudly for a cure?

Shrouded anxieties and shouted hopes
Determination willfully copes
Striving for balance with resolution
Purging away emotional pollution
Clarity of thought through miracles of perception
Strengthened by discipline and volition
Silencing dirges lamenting wrong
And then chanting out a whole new song

With love begins the transformation
The shift away from morose vexation
Through cracks in the surface, hope shines out
Coursing through the shell of fear and doubt
Melting the stone of seeming perdition
Dissolving the prison of this forged condition
Standing firm against the starkness
A shining beacon within the darkness

<u>Bye</u>

Although you are gone
Your mem'ry lives everywhere
Goodbye's never end

Call to Spring

When the Vernal Equinox has passed
The icy grip Winter has on us will not last
A golden light pierces though the clouds
The Sun breaks away from Its dark, chilly shrouds
Dark gray clouds give way to creamy white
Daytime grows longer, overcoming the night
Warm and cool spring showers fall
Now's the awakening, hear the call
Lord, we await Thee, in clear blue skies
Come wipe the haze of Winter from our eyes

Candle Shine

Upon a waxen pedestal
There is born a spark
That brightens to maturity
And shines away the dark

A curved and orange body
Red ribbons in blonde hair
Blue feet she stands upon
And waves in the air

Twinkling in the darkness
She illuminates
Dancing in the blackness
Waves and undulates

Candlelight in the tower
The castle's fast asleep
She dances through the night
And her secrets she will keep

Candy Kiss

Your lips, I wonder, how they taste
They must be sugar, for your voice is sweet
Your breath is fragrant of confection
Your candied lips should prove a treat

Will you cater to my sweet tooth?
That is, if I'm behaving
But I can't promise just one kiss
Will satisfy my craving

Cats on a Couch

The cats cuddled on the couch
Nuzzling noses into one another
Their wide eyes taking each other in

Cuddling and snuggling
Warmth and fuzziness
Stroking hair and scratching chins

Stretching and curling
Crooning and purring
A feline song and dance

Softly caressing
In loving embrace
A sweet cats' romance

<u>Change</u>

Holding on tightly
But nothing is permanent
Only change remains

Cloaked Reality

Your face is cold
But your eyes are warm
Which belies your heart?
Are you still in love?
Or have you buried it
Beneath a heavy blanket
Of numb self-deception?

Cloaked reality
Stifled by too many cares
And hidden behind thick walls
To protect the vulnerable truth
Feelings denied, betrayed
And nearly forgotten
A tragedy of love

It is not gone
It is never lost
Your love lies like hot coals
Buried beneath the ash
Waiting to be fanned to flame
Again

Come, Lord, Come

Come, Lord, Come
Come claim Thy Bride
The Virgin, the Maiden
Our Lady waits inside

Come, Lord, Come
Come claim Thy Bride
Return Thy Light to us
Not in Winter hide

Come, Lord, Come
Come claim Thy Bride
Come share Thy secrets
In Thy people confide

Come, Lord, Come
Come claim Thy Bride
Teach us the laws
By which we must abide

Come, Lord, Come
Come claim Thy Bride
And in Thy chariot
Across the sky ride

Come, Lord, Come
Come claim Thy Bride
We await Thy return
Filled with love and pride

Come, Lord, Come
Come claim Thy Bride
Come, Lord, Come
She'll be Your guide

She waits at the gates of Spring
Once you join Her inside
You shall be crowned King
And over Summer You'll preside

Come, Lord, Come
In Your Godly stride
Come, Lord, Come
With Your blazing pride

She waits with hair a-flowing
Her beauty cannot hide
She reflects Your glowing
Poised to turn the tide

Come, Lord, Come
Come claim Thy Bride
Come, Lord, Come
Into Springtide!

Contrast

Light shines more brightly out of darkness
Peace, an oasis among violence
The rainbow's more appreciated beyond the storm
Music rings sweeter in silence
Home holds more comfort since being away
Affection's more appreciated having gone without
Love warms more sweetly from cold loneliness
A shower of kisses after the drought

<u>Cronos</u>

Old age and Karma
Bear the Lantern of insight
You are Father Time

Crossroads

A man sits on a stone at the crossroads
Looking at the ground
There's a post at his back with arrows on it
Showing which way to go
He goes nowhere; chaining himself to the stone; no decision
Afraid to quest, afraid to leave
Afraid to tarry, afraid to stay
Clouds stagnate in the sky, suffocating the blue

How long will he sit there?
How long will he last?
Will he move on his own?
Will he be taken away?
Will he die, chained to his stone
(He's no Prometheus)

He breaks the chains and lifts his head
The clouds break and blue shines through
He studies the post and its arrows
He stands on the stone and he turns;
Studying the roads, the paths his life can take
Not knowing where to go
Not liking his choices
Knowing they'll lead back here

So he blazes a new trail . . .

Crowned With Laurels

Inspired by heaven and crowned with laurels,
She is my favorite artist.
Combining all nine muses in one woman;
A wonder I never believed existed.

With Clio, she remembers ages past,
And Urania, she gazes at the starry sky;
She performs and worships with Polyhymnia,
And shares Erato's passion for love and romance;

A sense of humor to rival comedic Thalia
Balanced by Melpone's sense of tragedy;
Euterpe's love of music and song
Celebrated with Terpeschore's dance;

And with Calliope, she brings them all together
In an epic of artistic magnificence.

All she touches turns to art.
She inspires my soul and heart;
In paint, in clay, in fabric;
Her voice a song; her movement a dance.

Sculpted to perfection and painted masterfully,
She is my favorite work of art.
Combining all nine muses in one woman;
A treasure I never believed existed.

Cupid, Have Mercy!

Oh Cupid, have mercy!
Thy arrows fly fast
And stick deep.
Emotive tips intoxicate.
My heart swoons.

Oh Blind Archer!
Sweet Cherub of Love!
In your quiver of affection,
Have you a bolt for my beloved?
Charm her as you have me.

Oh, Son of Venus!
Aphrodite's Child!
If I must love,
Let me be loved.
And let it be true.

Dam My Eyes

Dam my eyes
To hold back the tears
Though the sorrow goes on
The pain perseveres
The water pools
Behind the block
Emotions held back
Behind door and lock
Tears gather strong
The reservoir swells
Impending disaster
This condition foretells
And still rain comes
Storm after storm
Tears & sighs
Swirl & swarm
The river grows higher
The level elevates
A drop trickles over
The mighty flood gates
And yet another
As the current grows strong
The dam grows weaker
In the emotional throng
The relentless river
Is brutal in force
And the sorrowful water
Prepares to take course
The dam slowly crumbling
The gates ever weakening
Under the force of the pressure

The waves greatly peaking
Cresting & falling
From hurting & caring
The river takes force
Breaking & tearing
And spraying o'er the edge
Comes the waterfall
And in its wake
The dam now falls
A tempest of passion
A whirlpool of fears
A rapids of emotion
A deluge of tears
Channeled down the valley
Reeking havoc in its path
Toppling villages
In its watery wrath
Survivors scatter
As they flee
But they are drowned
When they reach the sea

Desperately Shallow

Back-pedaling schemer
Trying to retract his
Brash proposition
In a desperately shallow attempt
To greedily obtain
What he does not deserve

Devyn

Devyn celebrates the
Emotion of the Muses.
Valet is he to their
Youngish ruses.
Nine are his mistresses!

Did I Dream?

Did I dream?
Or was it an apparition
That kissed me,
That I can still feel
Her lips on mine?
The whisper of her voice
Still echoes in my ears
The touch of her hand
Still tingles on my skin
Her haunting scent
Still lingers in my hair

Let me dream again!!

Dissolve

Transformed emotion
Anger and hatred and fear
Dissolve into tears

Do You Udrentansd?

Futstread
We try to elpixan
Waht it is we feel
But wrods fial
As we cohke on cenotncps
Ftiule to be esprxesed
By Wrods
Taht cna't seem to cevony
An acucatre dicrpseotin
Of waht's in the haret

Dream

Last night I had a dream
The sweetest dream I ever dreampt
And when I woke I knew
That in my sleep I wept
So I wished again to slumber
And once again I slept
And deep in my heart a secret
That has long a secret been kept
Materialized in my dreamscape
And into consciousness crept

Elements

From the East, I bring
The breath of life
The wind of change
Intellect & communication

From the South, I bring
The heat of passion
The fire of creativity
Courage & protection

From the West, I bring
The tides of emotion
The waters of birth
Love & intuition

From the North, I bring
The salt of prosperity
The soil of fertility
Stability & healing

The four quarters fold together
The Elements coalesce
And from their union
Quintessence, Akasha, Spirit!

Embrace

The night fog surrounds me
But it cannot hold me
I cannot hug the air
Emptiness fills me
Coldness chills me
As it kisses my skin and hair

My head, it spins
My heat, it sins
In my belly a beehive swarms
I cry to be embraced
Some warmth to taste
But loneliness has no arms

I draw my arms across my chest
Pulling them close in a futile test
Hoping the chill to erase
But I stay just as cold
For my arms cannot hold
Warmth in my own embrace

So I feel all the more alone
And as if I swallowed a stone
Heartbreak has no charms
With drops on my face
I cry for an embrace
But loneliness has no arms

Emissary

I sigh deeply and dream of affection
- Doting on the kiss, the caress, the embrace -
As delivered by an emissary of Aphrodisia

While I'm enamored by her beauty,
Surrendering to her charms,
I'm brought back in time
By constant recollection;
Reminiscing in a moment,
An unfading memory.

To dream, to caress, to feel
Soft warmth and tender touches

Ah, but it's just an elusive vision
As tangible as shifting smoke.

But . . .
With just one of her touches
My dreams become rewards!

Emotional Deluge

At devil's door The kiss of death Clouded thought Short of breath Hands that shake Palms that sweat Roll the dice Lose the bet Butterflies in stomach Anticipate Anxiety, tension Fear of fate Tingling sensation Shiver and shake Emotional deluge Peace at stake Arriving swiftly Like a wall Plunging deeply Feel the fall Hit the bottom Feel the pain Paranoia? Or just insane? The storm is over All is well No cause for alarm As I can tell Once again The cycle complete Once again The cycle repeats At devil's door The kiss of death Clouded thought Short of breath . . .

Empty Spaces

A thread of muslin leads me on
In the empty spaces when she's gone

Traces of anger, spotted with fears
Destitution, washed with tears

Rose petals, dried memories, that haunt me
Light fantasies, dried dreams, that taunt me

The smell of her perfume lingers in my hair
The scent of loneliness in the air

Left alone in an empty room
The spaces fill with ensuing gloom

Enchantress

A Welsh glamour drew me there,
Feelings condensing in my heart like morning dew.
Magic in the braiding & untangling of red hair,
Bewitchment in enchanted eyes' green hue.

She was a beauteous avatar of romance.
But oasis or mirage, a desert rain?
An apparition to tease and taunt my circumstance.
Did I stand in shadows, with a view to the end of
    pain?

She was Creiddylad, for which the Oak & Holly
Kings fought, to no avail, without letup.
She was my passionate folly
She was the bitter dregs of Llud's cup.

Enter: Winter

Biting frost,
And sounds like the whisper of several winds
Leaves, falling
As his touch, from the trees, the Green Man
    rescinds

Dark clouds,
Like ink stains hanging heavy in the sky
While above
Ice castles form, chilled & rising high

Snow falls
Sounding as notes from a host of broken bottles
Blanketing
Beneath its chilly shroud, the sleeping earth it
    coddles

Esoteric Lovers

Lord and Lady, Paragon of Lovers
A Wondrous lesson to Discover

Paradigm of Partnership
Archetypal Relationship

As Above, So Below
But we mortals learn so slow

Sadly few and far between
Have insight enough to glean

The Language of Secret Communication
Regretfully lost in translation

But there are those with Loving Bonds
Who are Spiritual and beyond

Who know the Ways of Scourge and Kiss
Who've felt the touch of Passion and Bliss

Who exercise Faith, Trust, and Grace
Who Celebrate Life in Divine Embrace

Who have passed from Initiation
Through the fires of Transformation

Hoping this Life Together is ample
To teach how to Love by example

Expression

You feel the power of my words
Melting you into a pool of bliss

Yet words fail to express
The vastness of my emotion
The depth of my love

Reach into my passion
And feel the heat

Touch my soul
It resonates with yours

Explore the depths of my heart
And know my sincerity

Go deep into your heart
And find my love there

Familiar Face

A Familiar face
Behaving like a stranger
Um...Do I know you?

Fell

To the beginning, let me trace
When I fell in love
And fell from grace

It was the moment I saw her face
I fell in love
And fell from grace

And so then we began the chase
And fell in love
And fell from grace

Caught each other in an embrace
Fell in love
And fell from grace

With fear we turned an about-face
We fell from love
We fell from grace

We stood alone in empty space
Without love
Without grace

And learned our love was not
misplaced
We fell in love
We fell with grace

Foolish Heart

What a fool I am
To taste paradise and not know its sweetness
To not appreciate this gift kindly given me
To be so cold with this warmth in my presence
To be so sad with happiness at my threshold
To be so lonely with love knocking at my door

What an angry man I am to scowl
To curse myself when you do bless
To say I hate my bitter life
When with love you grace it well
What a selfish man I am to want
And to take, and not to give

Oh what an ass I am to be
The way I am, how I behave
How cruel I am to treat you thus
To break your heart when you've done no wrong
What a child I am; crying this way
Feeling hurt, when I hurt you

Confused am I to not know
What I want and what I need
How can I heal your broken heart
When my own I cannot mend?
How can I wrong your gracious love
And expect you to forgive again?

For Papa

From beneath a tree
   At the center of the shire
Puffs of smoke rose
   From a stoked coal fire
Where iron was heated
   To a great cherry red
'Fore being shaped
   Upon the anvil head
Smitten and smythed
   To twist and to bend
To shape and to form
   To join and to mend
Though it wasn't only metal
   'Pon which he worked his spell
The Master Smith's alchemy
   Transformed us all as well
Now the forge grows cold
   With no one there to tend it
A sword lies broken
   With no blacksmith to mend it
Yet his spirit lives on
   Within all our hearts
What he has formed
   Let no one take apart

Genesis

Creation is the mystery of the Endless Void...

Deep in the waters of the Black Abyss
There lies the Crucible of Dreams
That bottomless Cauldron, teeming with stars
Where Ultimate Nothing becomes Infinite
Possibility

Bursting forth from Blackness like a supernova
The Womb of Chaos gives birth to Dancing Light!

Ghost of a Muse

Memories fade like morning mist
Intangible, as a dream upon waking
Stinging as a betrayal kiss
Empty as a love forsaken

Her image dances in my mind
A paragon of Womankind

Her voice echoes in my ears
I taste her absence in my tears

She's just a ghost of a muse
Haunting my soul
Is this vision just a ruse
To fill the creative hole?

The pain of a poet to lose
His goddess of inspiration
Is more than enough to produce
Feelings of frustration

She's gone, something remains
A bittersweet pain

The sweet aching within
Of most blessed sin

She just a ghost of a muse
Haunting my heart
The shadow of the one who's
Inspired my art

GODDE

Goddess & God
Opposite Equals
Divine Twins
Divine Union
Eternal Balance

<u>Grow</u>

Joy blooms where kisses are planted

Basking in the sunshine of our smiles
We sow the seeds of our relationship

Showered with love
We make each other grow

Hangover

What strange feeling is this
That's in my heart when I wake?
Is it sadness or bliss;
A delight or mistake?

It's a feeling of love
Yet a feeling of loneliness
It feels like fulfillment
Yet also emptiness

It's many things remembered
Yet many things unknown
It's embraces left wanting
And affections shown

It's a craving, an addiction
It's a feeling in her absence
A pining, a longing
That goes away in her presence

For I've gotten drunk on her smiles
Intoxicated by her eyes
And the after effects
Have been aching and sighs

And so I feel this way
When our time together is over
Having been drunk on her love
And left with a hangover

Haunted

All
that is
beautif
ul in
this
world
is dead
And their
animated
corpses mock
me
Tormenting my
existence
With the recollection
Of withered beauty, lost love,
And broken dreams

Hecate

Wise Grandmother
Queen of All Magick
Who stands at the crossroads
And stirs the Cauldron of Transformation
Hounds howl in your honor
We see your face in the Dark Moon
You are a stern parent
Guiding us to Wisdom

How Sad, My Friend, Your Fear

Curses! My pale-hearted friend
What sadness it is to see you
Crumble beneath the weight of the universe
How your mind clouds out hope
And gives cause to only augur disaster
Capricious, your discordant emotions dance
To the reckless tempo of your pounding heart
Dictated by that tyrannous master, fear
Who slays you from within, yet keeps anonymity
For the fearful seed, planted within flourished
And must be razed from the root
To cease the decay of integrity
How sad, my friend, your fear
That it has taken you from me

In the Chair

she kneels before Him, taking His hand
Lowers her eyes, hopes, He'll understand
she offers her love into His care
He caresses her cheek, so fair
And placing a finger under her chin
He tilts her head up towards Him
Beckoning her to surrender a kiss
she complies, He tastes her bliss
In His lap, she rests her head
Without words it all is said
He runs His fingers through her hair
she on his lap, Him in the chair

In Your Arms, I'm Home

No matter where we are
Your arms feel like home
Where I am safe and warm

No matter life's weather
I find shelter in your embrace
I find love in your face

And as long as we are together
No matter where we roam
In your arms, I'm home

But now you're so far away
And I am here alone
I want to go back home!

Oh how I miss my home!

Individual Child

As dust in schoolroom corners sits unnoticed by the
        children,
So does he
They treat him as if he was infected with some
        contagion
Yet he's the one who's immune

He idles alone, thinking,
While innocent-looking youths play like tigers in
        the school yard
He watches them dance like phantasms -
Unreal in their behavior, yet seemingly haunting
        this earth

No loss in this exclusion - He doesn't belong
He's different somehow, perhaps better
For this understanding crept into him early in life
And this gives him hope
And a light of love, yet more enduring
Than this missed childhood that runs out like sand
        before him
His time to shine will come!
Not as a follower, but as an individual!!

<u>Innocence</u>

You trusted your innocence
        To my safekeeping
                Vowed by flesh
                        Sealed with a kiss

      I protect it with my life

A virgin
        forever
              in my eyes

Into Madness Ride

The Noon sky is black
No Sun, Moon or stars
In the midst of attack
Yet no visible scars

Product of society
Caustic and bane
Well of anxiety
Eternal pain

Upon the pale horse
Into madness ride
Victim of the force
Burning inside

Talons of torture
Claw at my flesh
Imminent vulture
Awaits the wretch

Take your mount
Grab the reins
Add one to the count
Of the Insane

Kali

Dark Mother
Your appearance inspires fear in my heart
Dressed in stillness
Jeweled with silence
A visage of death

Dark Mother
Your love is strict
You love not the fearful
Not to punish, but to exalt

You bid me come
Be transformed
Rebirth awaits beyond

I swallow my fear
And approach with courage

The only way out is through

Keen for Autumn

"How beautiful it is," they say
Of all the autumn leaves
As they change from green
To orange, to red, to yellow, to brown
Beauteous, yes, I must confess it
Yet I marvel at the moroseness of it;
To be keen for the ocular signs of death
While the wind in the branches howls a keen for the
    dead
Can we be excused for this morbid fascination?
Indeed, if we remember the mystery:
"All that dies shall be reborn!
All that falls shall rise again!"

Know Thyself

Know thyself be the challenge
The ultimate test of time
To understand the mental reasons
To understand the emotional rhyme

Gazing into feeling waters
Delving into that strange pool
Where my voice drowns in thought
And currents run 'tween sage and fool

Turbulent waters reflect little
And reveal nothing that lies below
Still waters reflect deceptively
Shrouding the true undertow

Leaf

The breeze will always blow you

Like a leaf on the wind

You let
it carry you
away

Changing directions, never settling

And calling nowhere
home

When the wind blows on your back
Hold fast to the safety of your tree
Cling to his branches
And remain
Grounded

Leather Hug

The leather holds you
Safely in a tight embrace
Just like my strong arms

Leather Kisses

Firm in hand and soft of touch
Suede tendrils of black
In His clutch
Gently tickling her back
And lightly brushing
It never misses
Sensations rushing
Sweet stinging kisses

Left to Wonder

Passionate heart
Torn apart
Emotions asunder
Left to wonder:
Love or not?
Or just forgot?
Silently reflecting?
Or just neglecting?
False or true?
I don't, I do?
To be or not to be?
For eternity?

Living & Learning

I'm just a man
Here in this crazy world
Trying to take a stand
Not just do as I'm told

I make my mistakes
And make my advances
'Cause that's what it takes
Decisions and chances

Living and learning
Seeing with new eyes
As the Wheel is turning
Mature and grow wise

Longing

Parched
I hold out my empty glass
With no drop to grace it
The thirst lingers on

Yearning
With desire unmatched
Wishing for satisfaction
To extinguish this lust

Craving
To feed this emptiness
Satiate the appetite
An unfed hunger

Lost Sands

You can't stop the sands of time
It slips though your fingers
The best of times are lost
The worst of memories linger

And before you know it
The last grain is gone
And you're at the end
Of something you thought was long.

Love Drunk

Basking in the glow of our love
We lay in a warm embrace
The back of my hand, gently
Caressing the curve of your face

Dizzy from whispered words
Weak from multiple blisses
Chills from tender touches
And drunk on countless kisses

Love In The Mail

It's not easy
Stuffing love in an envelope
I can never find the right sized envelope
For the amount of love I want to send

How many stamps does it take to mail a hug?
How many stamps to mail a kiss?

I want to send my love to you
But it's not easy
Stuffing love in an envelope

Luna

My Lady has three faces
My Lady has three phases
She shows them each to me

Maiden
Of the Waxing Moon
You Bless things new
Mother
Of the Full Moon
You Bless things completed
Crone
Of the Waning Moon
You Bless things old

Queen of Heaven, Blessed Be!

Made Love to An Angel

Love was the sin
That put me in hell
I once was in heaven
Before I fell

Made love to an angel
Felt her blessed touch
No earthly belle
Could be so much

This celestial delight
Divine when she sings
Soft and light
As the brush of her wings

She could not stay
In this mundane place
As she flew away
I fell from grace

Malleable Truth

Truth is not stone
Not these days
Not anymore
For it seems that the truth
Is putty now

It's cheaper to make
And quicker to produce
And most importantly
It can be stretched
And changed and molded
And appear to be what it's not

Anyone can change the truth
To suit their needs
Because you can make anything
With Malleable Truth
Especially love and money!

Mars

God of War
Courage & Protection
Battle is Your playground
Strength, Your birthright
Victory, Your boon

Melting

Our eyes meet…
>We melt into smiles

We speak…
>Melting walls of ice

We touch…
>And we melt into one

We Kiss…
>And melt into puddles
>>At each other's feet

Mercury

Messenger of the Gods;
Of communication and travel;
Trickster you are,
Who bears the Caduceus
And the winged helm.
Remover of obstacles
Open the road
And lead the way!

Monsters

Monsters lurk deep in the dark of the mind
Ghosts haunt from the shadows of the past
Gruesome chains of perception bind us to them
Keeping us in the night

Drag the monsters out of the night
Bring the ghosts into the light
They cannot exist in the sun
They cannot exists with love

Love and Light will break the chains
Love and Light will set us free!

Moonlight Spell

Moonlight shadows and silver beams
Astral projections and lucid dreams
Dancing in the crystal light
Cast the circle at midnight
Calling in the Elements; four-fold
Invoking the God & Goddess of Old
Athame, Wand, Cup & Pentacle
Stone, feather, shell and candle
With incense, candle and with bell
Raise the energy, cast the spell

<u>Muse</u>

She inspires me
Everything she does is art
My beautiful muse

Muted Drums

Caution swims against excitement
The horses kept at the gate
Bucking and pacing to get out
Patience unable to wait

Hesitant to be heard
Our hearts beat like muted drums
Safely and secret
Waiting to burst into rhythm

Myself

I looked at myself in the mirror
And I saw in my eyes something
Someone I haven't seen for so long
It was myself, deep inside
Uneasy and disturbed, but still unyielding
In his fight to reemerge
And our eyes met - as one they are
Then we knew and understood each other
His strength, my fear, our battle
He pleaded to me with his eyes
I lowered my head in shame;
A tear rolled down my cheek
But he understands, I know
I have fought hard, he knows
I've wanted to quit so many times, I've tried
But he won't let me - not a chance
He wants to be again; new and improved
And when the fire burns down to ashes
He fans to coals to relight my passion
To strengthen me on my journey to freedom
I thank the Gods he's in here
Fighting for my life

Nocturnal Revelation

Listen ye who scoff at the will of heaven
And care less for prophecy than for profit
The Gods speak to those who listen. . .

Late. . . in the weary time of the night
When the large hours tumble into small and grow
    again
And. . . though burdened with a heavy head and
    tired eyes
Sleep comes uneasily, like water from stones

Yet...it is that stone, that Celestial orb
That tugs on waters and men's minds
Who has Her way with me
And wraps me, like Endymion into her spell

I sleep...and nestled in chaste Luna's silver arms
She carries me away to her Cancerous Realm
Where I, like the Crab, dance along the shore
Between the illusory water and the sands of
    consciousness

    The waves of the sea wash over me
    Bringing with them: revelation, dream, and
      prophecy

Diana watches over with Her silver bow drawn
Prepared to slay the ill, vexing phantasy
Which is insubstantial, like nightmare specters
And seldom yields prophetic fruit

With a mind open to the Astral
The Gods decant Their erudition
Gently, to my exposed soul
Which readily embraces Their wisdom

      The night grows old,
      And youthful morning will soon take over

With Aurora's first kiss
The oracles fade, the wisdom remains
Phoebus Apollo rides over the horizon
Shedding light and truth on all

Nyx

I am the stillness that swallows the sun
when the day grows old.
I am the shadow on the edge of twilight
as the wind turns cold.

I am the enchantress that beckons the world
to come slumber with me.
I am the void that embraces the stars
enfolded infinitely.

I am the spell that breaks with the dawn
as the earth wakes to light.
I am the silence that dies in the morn.
I am the darkness. I am Night.

Ocean Storm

The eyes seem perfect pools
The body, still as the surface of a pond
But within, the ocean of emotion
Tosses and turns in a tempest of feelings
Unstoppable currents of passion
The tide turns - ebb & flow
The storm surges, flooding the beach
Crashing upon the rocks
Creating storms in my eyes

Osun

Treasure of the Sweet Waters
Who delights in the mirror and comb
Offerings I make in yellow and white
Tasting the honey before presented
Sweetness for Sweetness

Poison Seed

Fear is a poison
Sinking in deep
Contaminating the mind

Draw out the poison
Out of the blood
Purify thoughts

Doubt is a weed
Entangling the heart
Choking out hope

Raze out the weed
Free the wilting hope
Plant optimistic seed

Pondering On A Weeping Child

What manner of man am I
That I am angered by a weeping child?
Am I annoyed by the disturbance;
This interruption of my peace,
Because children should be seen
And not heard; and be no bother to me?

Is it because it pains me
To see such innocence troubled
By the tiniest of trials
And fear for the young life
Unaware of what pains await
In the terrible years ahead

Or is it that I am jealous
Not only of the simplicity of the cause
But also of the freedom to express it
The liberty to exclaim discontent
And demand to be heard
And to command love and comfort
And receive it unconditionally

Private Longing

Private longing and sweet daydreams
Play in my mind like movie scenes
While tears of joy and tears of pain
Mingle together; a bittersweet rain.
Secret desires remain silent thoughts
Reveling my hidden emotions naught.
Hopes fading like autumn leaves.
The shattered, abandoned dream; it grieves.
My heart, swept out with a broom,
Leaving just an empty storeroom.

Raging Celestial

Raging celestial influences
Coursing through the sky
Catch us in their current
It's useless to defy
Aspects and retrogrades
Transits and returns
To survive the rapids
Ride the tide, we learn

Reflected Glow

The Sun Lord shines his love upon his Lady Moon
Which in turn makes her glow.
She reflects his love back unto Him
And thus returns the loving so.

I gaze into my lover's eyes
And she gazes, fondly, back at me.
I see my reflection in her adoring eyes
And, in mine, she herself sees.

Reflected into infinity
One inside the eyes of the other
Back and forth the love is returned
From lover unto lover

Love, in the face of the loved one, shows
For love, like the Moon, is a reflected glow.

Reflecting in Nocturne's Mirror

What are these visions that come to me
While submerged in the shimmering pool of sleep?
Are they merely mental debris, bobbing like corks
In the boundless waters of unconsciousness,
Or childish fantasies devised in the
Unconscious playground of the sleepless mind?

How many memories are accumulated in sleep?
How many lessons experienced in the guise of a
dream?
What truths are revealed by the unfolding shadows
That open like bright lotuses from muddy water
As we live lifetimes in each nightly slumber
Beneath the dark, heavy blanket of morphia.

Resurrected

Your eyes always wound me
And they never miss
I die with your touch
Resurrected by your kiss

Rhymes Unread

I've tried to write this poem two or three times now
It doesn't seem to get any less hard
I'm not as great of a poet as you might think
I'm not a great wordsmith like many a bard
The truth is I just write how I feel
Letting my emotions mingle with ink
Sometimes the poems are masterpieces
And sometimes they just stink
And many times I crumple them up
And toss them on the floor
And wonder why I bother writing
If my ability is so poor
But with each flawed page I crumple
And toss away in a ball
There's another feeling left untold
Another unexplained tear left to fall
And so I'd come to the conclusion
That I'll continue to write what I feel
Because it's in this way
That I can express and heal
and feelings are a precious thing
Though over-plentiful they seem to me
They are the things that make me human
Though painful they often seem to be
But what's more painful is the fact
That I fear to share these lines with you
And they speak only to the page where they live
No one but myself to view
Or into the fire they consume themselves
As the passion consumes me within
For it's my unexpressed feelings that burn
And that no one has read them, that is the sin

R.I.P.

Here lies trust
Laid to rest among the dust
Done to death by lust

Romance On Your Lips

Oh, how I yearn
To whisper in your ear!
Oh how the passion burns
Behind smiles and tears!

Intoxicating words;
Drunkenness in the air,
Gliding like birds
And tangling in your hair.

Take this wine from me
- But drink it in small sips
For it may make you dizzy;
Intoxicating romance on your lips.

Rose Asunder

A rose falls scattered
Tossed without care
Love lies shattered
Its pieces cast everywhere
Randomly littering
The mud and the grass
Petals glittering
Like crimson glass
Untainted by mud
Stay vibrant and bright
As passionate blood
On the darkest night

Rubble

The truth is betrayed
All that I believed crumbles
To uncertainty

Somewhere Under The Rainbow

Gray sky and silver drops
Washing away the color
Leaving a black and white world
Dull, dark, depressing

But then the storm subsides…

A rainbow cuts through the drab
Painting all below with light
Bringing color again to all
Oz on Earth

Speaking Kisses

Lips can speak without uttering a word
Yes, silent lips can be heard
Two lips, tightened gently into a pucker
Pressed against the lips of another
The message is clearly conveyed
And not a word has been said

Spoken Bullets

Words carry so much pain
Spoken bullets to the soul
The mind forgets, the heart remembers
Verbal razors take their toll

    Every insult an arrow
    Flying swift and sticking deep

This dagger stuck into my heart
Was spoken from the mouth of thee
Sticks and stones may break my bones
But words will deeply scar me

Stars

The universe spins in concentric circles
As I try to contemplate its intangible visions.
Gazing at the smoky backwaters of heaven
And the celestial dancing patterns augury,
I read my destiny,
Written out for me
On the velvet backdrop of night.

Sub Rosa

"Master I come seeking
The knowledge nature knows."
To which the wise man said,
"It lies beneath the rose.
I cannot give you the truth,
You must find it on your own.
Listen to the wind, the trees,
The plants, the stars, the stones.
I cannot tell you
Where this knowledge grows,
For the seed of this enlightenment
Lies beneath the rose.
The secrets of the Witch,
Who by solemn oath hath sworn,
Are not simply handed
To one so recently born.
The cycles of the cosmos,
That into each other weave,
Do not simply present themselves
To one who's foolish and naïve.
No, the young one does not understand
For he has not acquired with age
The experience and lessons
The forge the wisdom of the sage.
If I were to hand you
The answers for which you yearn
Then I would deny you the understanding
And nothing you would learn.
The student seeks the answers,
And the secrets WILL unfold

When the Gods see fit to inspire you.
Of this you have been told.
Sow the seeds of the seeker,
For without it no knowledge grows.
And when the petals unfurl
The answers will lie beneath the rose.

Suffering

Sanity leaking out
Under the martyr's mask
Fear multiplies within
Fingers grip in agony
Endless inferno burning
Reason not to live
Insanity reaping rewards
Never showing mercy
God forbid

Sunrise

The Heavens cry
In the night sky
Oh, woe to be me!

In the grip of fear
I shed a tear
Oh! When will I be free?

The storm clears
And dawn nears
I long to see the light

The Sunrise
Before my eyes
Shining on me bright

The dawn brakes
My heart aches
Crumble all away

My body thrives
I'm alive
Yet another day

The azure sky
Fills my eyes
With electric blue

I drink it in
The liquid wind
And taste the morning dew

The cool, fresh air
Blows through my hair
And makes me feel alive

Talking in our Sleep

In a silent slumber
Stillness settled inside
And finding blissful sleep
My mental chatter died

Then something came
From out of the dark
A flash of light
An elusive spark
It was a voice
I knew so well
What did she say?
What did she tell?
Words she spoke
Of such import
But the message
Alas was so short
A fleeting moment
And it was gone
The dream was lost
And it was dawn

What was the message
That she had sent?
What were her words,
What sentiment?

Maybe she heard
My heart's own decry
In her slumber
She had heard me

Do our dreams reveal
The secrets we keep?
Perhaps our hearts
Are talking in our sleep

Tapestry

As we strive towards desire
We spin a thread
And when or threads cross
We twist and tangle
Our threads together
Creating a tapestry of woven wishes
That reaches towards the stars
Or as a blanket
That keeps us warm
When we lie down to dream

Taste

Naked, you lie
submissive; trusting much
Breath on your skin
An invisible touch
That heralds the coming of kisses
Chills parade your body
Anticipating blisses
My lips caress your curves
A plan of pleasure's fashion
The dance of my tongue
Tasting your passion.

Temperance

Loving my lady
With a firm and gentle touch
Passion and pleasure

Temptation

Don't let temptation
Carry you away

Don't lose your way
For a moment of weakness

What a terrible cost
True love lost
Gambled away for shallow pleasure

The Artist

He dreams.
He walks in color down a black and white street.
Wishing to paint a world of vibrant beauty.
Hopes, just a flash in the pan;
Fleeting hues, intangible as shifting smoke.

He dreams in color.
A reprieve from his dull black and white life;
A temporary parole from his monochrome sentence;
A sentence without color; no adjectives; plain;
Just black ink on a white page.

He thinks in poetry.
Painting pictures with words,
Penning colorful metaphors with depth and
perspective;
Blending tones, tints and hues.

He shades them
From the critical editors of his life
Who cut and paste them to conform.
Sheepishly he hides them in the shadows.
Censoring his color in a black and white world.

He censors himself
Dims his bright colors
In a dull, dark world.

So he dreams...
He dreams in color.

The Cards

Two-fold "The Fool"
Man & Woman
Following "The World"
"The Magician" is drawn

A Page with a Cup
A Knight on a horse
Three Cups times three
A wish comes true

A King with blue eyes
Counselor & healer
Hurt by life
That's me and you

"The Hanged Man" are we
Sacrificed for love
And with "The Tower" rebuilt
Ten Cups are afoot

And "The Sun" awaits
To greet "The Fools"
At the end of the path
The final card.

The Colors of Godde

The Divine Light radiates
Shining down from Heaven
Upon the dark Earth

Crystalline rays
Filter though the Mundane Prism
Creating heavenly Hues

All of Creation is Illuminated
By the Vibrant Spectrum
of the Colors of Godde

The Funny-Looking Thing

…And God looked out over the blackness and said,
   "Let there be light!
"Whoa," he said, "Couple it with dark, 'cause that's
   just too bright!
"Now let there be earth, and sky and mountain and
   sea;
"And let there be heaven (that'll be for me).
"Let there be plants and let there be trees,
"Let there be animals named from A to Z."
Six days later, God looked down and said,
"This thing's funny-looking, I must be out of my
   head."
But then he added harmony to his creation
And once more he looked down with elation.

The Gift

I have something for you
A simple little gift
That'll put a smile on your face
And make your spirits lift
It will make you the richest woman in the world
Yet physical value it has not
It is, indeed, a priceless gift
For price is has naught
It's not made of sterling silver
It's not made of gold
It has no precious stones in it
It can't be bought or sold
It won't fade or tarnish
It won't chip, crack or peel
You can't reach out and touch it
But it is very real
It has no fragrant petals
It has no stem or leaves
It's not an article of clothing
It has no buttons or sleeves
It has no scent, taste or sound
It has no shape or size
You can't taste or hear it
You can't see it with your eyes
It can't be manufactured
By machine or handmade
For if it doesn't come naturally
Its preciousness would fade
So please accept this gift
That I freely give to you
My respect, loyalty, & trust
And my love that's true

The Girl With The Sage Eyes

Her youthful face can't disguise
The lifetimes reflecting in her eyes…
The girl with the sage eyes

She's been born so many times
She has spun so many rhymes…
The girl with the sage eyes

Young her body may be
But her soul has history…
The girl with the sage eyes

Don't be fooled by her tears
She is wise beyond her years…
The girl with the sage eyes

The Lover

Dinner for one and candle light
Soft, romantic music on a Friday night

The lover is deafened by the silent phone
The lover sits at home alone

In front of the fire, nice and warm
From his eyes, a tempest; a storm

A vase of flowers; pink and red
"To my love," the little card read

But with no one to give them to
They wither away, it's sad but true

Gentlemanly manners & chivalrous tasks
But a princess this prince charming lacks

Poetic acclamations & Shakespearean praise
But the only answer this poet gets is "nay"

Dancing a slow dance, the lover moans
For the lover, sadly dances alone

The Machine

The Machine slowly lurches forward
Through the blackness
Through the red
Through the razors
Through the thorns
Its flesh is ripped
But continues to run
Clanking and turning
Wheezing and coughing
putter . . . putter . . . putter
But moves on
On its last leg
Low on oil
Cranks turn
Gears grinding
Systems over-loading
Maximum overdrive
The Machine *painfully* lurches forward
Forward in agony
The wounds reopen
Sweat stings inside
Way past warranty
Parts discontinued
The Machine tries to lurch forward
Ready for the scrap heap.

The Muses

The Muses are nine as one
They are all of one mind
And, dancing, they are of one body
As they turn, leap, and wind
And, as a chorus, of one voice
Harmonizing as they sing
And they are all of one heart
In passionate art rejoicing
They are all of one spirit
Daughters of thundering Jove
Individual in their talents
Sisters united by love.

The Poet Is...

The poet is born of art
Lives on beauty reflected
Dies, consumed by passion
And by love, is resurrected

The Poet's Crux

Poets are dreamers, flying so high
Feet on the ground, head in the sky

Reaching for the sun, the poet crashes
Wings of his dreams turned to ashes

Hot and cold, the poet sways
Doting on temperate days

The blood is hot which feeds his passion
And poetry's bred by this heat's fashion

With ardorous blood, he fills his well
And dips his quill; his tale to tell

The Poet Who Dreamed

There once was a poet who dreamed
Was True Love as it once seemed?
  If a heart had wandered
  And affection was squandered
Could that Love still be redeemed?

The Willow Tree

The Willow Tree was beautiful
Among the other trees of the forest.
He sought her companionship again.

He moved beneath the droopy tree
And immediately felt the comfort of her embrace;
The protection of her branches

She felt like home.

He paused for a moment...
Did she speak to him?
Silence...

He snuggled himself into her roots,
Finding his resting place,
And kissed the scar upon her trunk.

The sweet scent of moist earth and green leaves
Soothed his tired emotions.
He fell silent...

In the stillness, he listened...
Waiting for the Willow to Whisper...

The World Opens Up

I sit alone at dawn, under a tree
And gaze the sky to see what I can see

And the sky reveals eternity
And the tree gently embraces me
The world opens up to me

I stand on a mountain, watching the sunrise
Letting the gold light into my eyes

Basking in the light of the sun
And the day that has just begun
The world opens up to me

Lying in the grass in an open field
Waiting for the mysteries to be revealed

I see a bud blossom into a rose
Its perfume gently tickles my nose
The world opens up to me

Gazing up at the night time sky
And its vastness overwhelms my eyes

The stars shimmering though the night
And the full moon shining down on me bright
The world opens up to me

Because I have eyes willing to see
The world shows its beauty to me
The world opens up to me

Three Wishes

I wish I could forget
The touch of your sweet love
And make myself numb

I wish I didn't care
About you at all
Apathy is bliss

I wish I could hate you
And defeat the helpless feeling
of loving you against my will

To Get Together

To get her
To let her
To befriend her
To meet her
To amour her
To be sweet to her
To pursue her
To charm her
To love her
To do for her
To risk for her
To dare for her
To share with her
To care for her
To woo her
To romance her
To dance with her
To take that chance for her
To befriend each other
To meet each other
To amour each other
To be sweet to each other
To pursue each other
To charm each other
To love each other
To do for each other
To risk for each other
To dare for each other
To share with each other
To care for each other
To woo each other

To romance each other
To dance with each other
To take that chance for each other
To meet together
To be sweet together
To learn together
To yearn together
To grow together
To show together
To share together
To care together
To pursue together
To do together
To take that chance together
To find romance together
To dance together
To get her
To get
Together
To love each other
To love
Together

True

True love isn't expressed in words
Every glance, caress, and sigh tell the tale
A dance of deeds is love in motion

True love isn't holding hands,
It's touching souls!

TRUST

Tell me all your dreams
Reveal your secrets unto me
Unveil your hidden self
Submit your heart to me
They'll be safe in my keeping

Two Figures

Two figures stand
Face to face
Gazing at the each other
As into a mirror
Themselves reflecting
In the eyes of the other
The other in themselves
Complimenting same
Bringing out different
Separately together
United in diversity
So alike
So different
So mutual
Bringing out the same
Complementing different
Two figures standing
Side by side
Hand in hand
Arm in arm
Walking their separate paths
Together...

<u>Trees</u>

I'm a tree-hugger
Willow, Rowan, and Hazel
How I love my trees

Unbroken Silence

Waiting...
      Not to end

Empty...
      Not to be filled

Stillness...
      Not to be shaken

Heavy...
      Not to be lifted

Quiet...
      Not to be broken

Vast...
      Not to be crossed

Anticipating...
      Not to be quenched

Words...
      Not to come...

Unfeeling Creatures

What unfeeling creatures these modern mortals are
They spend their loves in the offices and cars
How can they be untouched by the sadness of the
world?
How can warm-blooded beings learn to be so cold?
Undisturbed by the horrors that other will commit
They continue unfazed by all the worst of it
How can they love with emotion forged of steel?
Wills of ice and hearts of stone; it's all so unreal
In this modern moving world, man's become
machine
Not a single one remembers where we've been
And all the lonely souls that compassionately walk
the earth
Suffer in this sadness that was once a world of mirth

Voice

A voice from within
Shouts to be heard through chaos
Devyn, I love you

Waking Up From A Dream

I drift to sleep
And start to dream
My heart did weep
Or so it seemed
That in my dream
She appeared
My faced beamed
With her near
I held her hand
Her skin was warm
And we would stand
In each other's arms
Having her there
Touching her face
Stroking her hair
My pulse starts to race
With love in my heart
And peace in my head
I wake with a start
Lying in my bed…
Alone

War on the Borders

Lost in a strange but familiar wilderness
I stood on the edge of thought and feeling
Where desolated wastelands met the dark unknown
And the landscape was scorched by war on the
      borders

An unquiet silence blanketed me as I listened
To the distant thunder of an approaching storm
Apprehension stirred in my belly
To stand in wait as anticipation does

Courage stretched, though buried
Beneath shades of frustration
Masked by anger, weakened by fear
And stained with lingering taints of sadness

Passion flared, stoked by the winds of change
And threatened to consume the very tissue that bred
      it
Burning hot with a lust for action

The world stood poised on that moment...

With a twist of fate and a calming breath
Emotions were tamed back to their cages
Peace and perspective appeared out of meditation
Clearing the way for wisdom and inspiration

Bowing my head, I prepared to scry
Into the dying embers of a final fire
Searching for answers longed for
And a sign of what's to come

What Cruel Trick

What cruel trick of perception
Makes strangers of lovers
And intimacy covers
With a veil of deception?

What He Could Not Tell Her

He thought that he could tell her anything,
But, for fear, there was something he couldn't.

He could reveal his darkest secrets to her
Without shame.

He could bear his soul to her
Without feelings of vulnerability.

He could speak to her of his follies
Without embarrassment.

He could speak of his dreams
Without feeling foolish.

What he could not tell her
Was that he loved her.

Whispers

What secret's revealed
In the rustling of leaves?
The willow whispers

Who Wakes Up The Sun

Who wakes up the Sun
On a cold Winter's morn?
Who dries away His tears
After a thunderstorm?
When He dies in Autumn's fall
Who sees that He's reborn?

It's His children who dance
His children who sing
His children who nurse Him
From Winter to Spring
And for His children
The Summer He'll bring!!

<u>Wounds</u>

Reaching deep behind the shield
She touches wounds, yet unhealed
Carved in his heart, by her hand
Still she doesn't understand
That pain that hides behind his smile
Is pain that lives by her denial

He winces discretely at her touch
While secretly loving her much
Simultaneously fearing of
The sting of unrequited love
As she denies him of his need
And the wounds continue to bleed

Written

We have wills written in stone
But our journey is written in the stars

Regret, written in our tears
Promises, written in the dark

Time is written in sand
Mem'ry's written in smoke

Passion, written in our blood
Love, written on our hearts

Adoration, written in our eyes
Longing, written in our sighs

Desire's written in our kiss
Pleasure, written on our flesh

You feel the tenderness, written in my hand
I see compassion written on your face

Secrets are written on your breath
Hope, written in your smiles

Change is written on the wind
But our destiny, written on our soul!

Yarn

My mind is a tangled ball of yarn
Many different colors

I can't find the ends
To undo the knot

Yemoja

Swaying like a wave
You dance upon the sea
A star on the horizon
Decorated with shells
And enrobed in blue and white

Loving Mother of the Ocean
I am your child

Zeus

Thunder Lightning and Rain
Father of the Gods
The Eagle be Your eyes
Throne of Olympus

Zombie

Living dead, am I
I have died a thousand times
Murdered by your words

Devyn Barat

Devyn Barat, resides in northern New Jersey where, in addition to being a poet, he also makes spiritual blends of incense and teaches classes on various spiritual and metaphysical topics for his business, Everything Akasha.

www.magickalpoet.com

I began writing in kindergarten to impress a cute girl. By the fourth grade, I was writing scripts, short stories, poetry and lyrics. The need to create and express has always been in my blood, but the mediums always seemed to elude me. Words were my only outlet.. I think in poetry. Unfortunately I can't speak the way I think, and if I didn't get it out, I'd explode. With pen and paper, I express this passion.

I find inspiration in the enjoyment of the arts and the study of mythology, metaphysics, religion, spirituality, and alternative lifestyles. I often attempt to bind these together with a common thread, illustrating universality.

My favorite poets are William Shakespeare and a long list of song writers (lyrics are poems set to music) including Ian Anderson, Jewel Kilcher, Jim Morrison, Paul O'Neil, Shel Silverstein, and many many more.

Please visit our web site to preview these exciting authors.
www.crystaldreamspub.com

Elizabeth Gibbs
Breath of Life-
$10.00

Ross Barber
Assassin-
$12.00

James Graves
Aftermath I-
$13.00

Phillip C. Beebe
A Stab in the
Back-
$10.00
Beyond the
Edge-
$10.00

Mark Haeuser
Hunters of the
Shadows-
$13.00

Jerry B. Pozner
Monkey
Pudding-
$12.00

Vladimir
Beregovoy
Hunting Laika
Breeds of Russia
$12.00

Nicole Givens-
Kurtz
The Soul Cages-
$13.00
Browne
Candidate-
$12.00

Andrea Bikfalvy
The Junkyard
Club-
$10.00

Keith Loines
Embracing the
Broken Spiral -
$11.00

John H. Burns
First Bite-
$10.00
Hidden
Treasures-
$10.00

Ed "Hawk"
Markow
Reflections of
Soaring - $11.00

Sarah
Schwersenska
The Soul of
Elizabeth-
$10.00

In Your Face
Erotica-
$11.00
Sylence
Campbell
Stirring the Sky –
$10.00

Julie Carda
Portal to Love-
$14.00

Weslynn
McCallister
Prophecies of the
Ancients-
$13.00

Clay Lamberton
Students
Schools Out-
$10.00
Who Let the
Cougars Out-
$10.00

Morris Striplin
Backwater-
$12.00
Grey Meadows,
P.I.-
$10.00
Also Available in
Hard Cover
$19.95

T. W. Miller
Bloody Mary-
$10.00

Rod Summitt
When Pasts
Collide-
$12.00

Jack J. Ward
Shadowland
Theater-
$11.00

CRYSTAL DREAMS
PUBLISHING

Quantity	Title/Author	Price

Subtotal _____

$2.50 US – 1st book $.100 each additional book
$3.50 International   Shipping and Handling _____

Total _____

☐ Enclosed check
☐ Please bill my Credit Card   ----   Card Number
   ☐ Master Card
   ☐ Visa   _____
   ☐ American Express   _____
   ☐ Discovery   _____
   ☐ Other   _____
                             _____

**Merchandise will not be shipped when paying by check, until the check
clears. All returned checks are subject to a $25.00 return check fee.**

Mail To:
W1227 East County Rd A
Berlin, WI 54923